HOW TO WIN A NOBEL PRIZE

A Stay-at-Home Mum's Guide

Published by Heliconia Press
(An imprint)

ISBN 10 : 981-05-6537-2
ISBN 13 : 978-981-05-6537-4

Artwork by MJ Ellis

Printed in Singapore on 100% post-consumer waste recycled paper.

Part of the proceeds from the sale of this Guide will be donated to UNICEF.

For my children

"Perhaps it is difficult to rouse women; they are long-suffering and patient, but now that we are roused, we will never be quiet again."
(Emmeline Pankhurst)

Being A Stay-at-Home Mum

I genuinely believe that giving up my career to be at home with the children was the best decision I ever made. After all, what could be more wonderful than being there for that first step, first word and first day at school?

What could be more rewarding than nurturing our young, developing their potential and sending them out into the world as responsible and thoughtful members of society?

And then, of course, there are those *other* days…

*"I know I have the body but of a weak and feeble woman;
but I have the heart and stomach of a King…"*
(Queen Elizabeth I)

Chapter 1 – Why a Nobel?

With all those bedtimes, bath times and mealtimes, school
runs and playdates, ballet and piano classes, homework
and holidays – a mother has to be on her toes just to keep
the children fed, happy, dressed and punctual.

If you are anything like me, a lot of the other time (and
there is not much of it) is spent on a quest for adult
conversation (which usually ends up revolving around
the kids). Or, failing that, is spent slumped in front of
the television.

The problem with this lifestyle is that, at some stage,
the children find their own friends, take the bus to the

cinema, skip the piano lessons and we mothers have a future on our hands. And for the first time in a long time, it is our future and not theirs. This is the point when we discover that we have a bad haircut, are 5kgs heavier than before the birth of our first child and have no life beyond the kids. To add insult to injury – our husbands, who have continued working as the sole breadwinner in all those years we were potty-training the children, are hitting a peak in their careers. They are looking good, feeling good, their golf games are getting longer and their secretaries are looking younger.

And they have no idea what we are complaining about – we've been whining for years about not having any time for ourselves – and now some free time frees up and the first thing we do is complain.

If, like me, you gave up a good job to stay at home with the kids, you will no doubt be feeling particularly aggrieved at this point. The problem – one of them – with the society we live in right now is that it is structured by men. As such, if we had some sort of career and took some time out to be at home with the children, we're stuffed.

It is almost impossible to pick up where we left off. First and foremost, we have forgotten pretty much everything we used to know about the job. It is possible that, like riding a bike, it all comes back after a while. Well, I've tried that. Not the job, the bike – it's pretty damn wobbly those first few hundred yards – and I leapt off at the first sign of traffic.

Even if someone gives us a job, everyone our age is a senior manager or a director or retired. People who used to fetch the tea are now our peers – except that they are younger, more energetic and slimmer. And, as they managed to have adult conversation in those years we were slouching in front of the television, their brains are still intact as well.

Nobody in management takes us seriously because, having once given up our careers in the best interests of the children, we're clearly not committed enough. We will be passed over for promotion, paid less than the next guy and treated with a pseudo-sympathetic air, as if falling off the career ladder was an unfortunate accident which might have happened to anyone but didn't – it happened to you and me – poor things.

So the best case scenario – for us stay-at-home mums – is that we will eventually rejoin the workforce in our former jobs or something similar and will probably spend the years until retirement moving sideways or going nowhere.

The worst case scenario is that we continue to be at home. We start living our lives vicariously through our children and spend a lot of money trying to maintain our youth – from now on it's all Botox and bum tucks. After a while, the children start to get embarrassed because we're trying to dress like our eldest daughter and they stop bringing their friends home. None of it works – we move out of the family home, the secretary moves in – it's all over. At this point, and it is very late in the day, we have to start rebuilding our lives from scratch. It is not going to be easy.

I am willing to concede that I may have exaggerated the bleakness of the future to make a point!

No doubt there are stay-at-home mums who are perfectly capable of rejoining the workforce and clawing their way back to the top of the heap. There might even be a few mothers out there who are blissfully content with the status quo and have no idea what I am talking about when I mention the difficulties of being a stay-at-home mum and the frustration of not being able to find any sort of acceptable work-life-children balance.

But when I look around, I am convinced there are a lot of women just like me. Women who *don't regret for a moment* their choice to stay at home with their young children. But who don't understand why the price of doing so has to be so high.

A lot of my women friends are showing signs of being only too aware of the potentially dismal future ahead of us stay-at-home mums when the kids are grown. A few have started exercising furiously. Others are having their fourth or fifth child. There is nothing particularly wrong with that. Nothing, that is, unless we mothers are having more children as an excuse not to confront a future without a needy newborn prop to make us feel worthwhile.

A few friends have started talking about some day, "when the kids are older", "training as something else". Non career-oriented jobs are a favourite. Among the ideas I have heard include re-training as a mid-wife or a plumber, designing comfortable yet attractive shoes and inventing sexy maternity bras. There is nothing objectionable about any of these ideas. I would love a pair of those shoes and we always need a good plumber. However, the generators of these ideas, with a bunch of kids each, are all women with stacks of work experience and professional qualifications. On top of that, all of them worked for years before quitting for the sake of the children.

I might add that none of their proposed alternative plans have actually come to fruition. There is no particular surprise in this. These are smart women flailing around trying to avoid the fate I have outlined above. In their hearts, they know full well that their previous careers are shot. The kids are growing up all too quickly. They need to work through their options. Nothing is feasible. The ideas being tossed up are the equivalent of a UN Security Council resolution on Israel – put out there on principle to be shot down.

As for me, having railed against the fates and bought every glossy magazine with articles along the lines of "How to raise the perfect family while working 24/7" (in case you are wondering, only in a parallel universe), I have finally concluded that I would not go back to my previous career even if I could. Really I wouldn't. Not even if they came along carrying bags of money and begged. Ok, maybe then! But it hasn't happened. And I genuinely don't want to go back to that commercial culture where value is judged only in dollar terms and being a 'team player' depends on how much you can drink with your bosses and colleagues before keeling over.

Having kids may not have changed my value system – but it has certainly re-arranged my priorities. It has always been my aim to do some "good" with my life. I am sure it is the same with many people. But I was quite happy to postpone that moment. As and when I had made enough money, influenced enough people, finished ordering my personal universe to my satisfaction – then I would turn my attention to good works. Having children changed all that.

Individual selfishness when exercised on a global scale leads directly to the end of the world as we know it. Without children – this is a consequence we can live with. After all, things are unlikely to get really bad in *our* lifetimes. At the very minimum, we appear to be prepared to *risk* the worst possible outcome to the greatest number of people.

An airy reliance on top-down solutions keeps the panic

at bay. If global warming gets really serious, our leaders will do something about it or human ingenuity will save the day. (Just stop a moment and picture George W. if you believe that). These defence mechanisms of the usual 'head in the sand' variety push away that nasty sinking feeling when you watch the latest disaster on CNN. Children change that too.

If you are a childless thirty-something with a professional job, on a business trip somewhere, watching the news in a posh hotel room – your most likely reaction to scenes of malnourished children in sub-Saharan Africa or injured children in Lebanon, is to donate, or at least plan to donate, some money to UNICEF. By the next morning, rushing for a breakfast meeting in the lobby and wondering whether your dry-cleaned suit is going to turn up in time, even the good intentions have probably dissipated. Children change all that too.

As every mother knows, it is just too easy to imagine your own children in that situation. Even if you can block that thought, in my experience, mothers have a genuine empathy for *every* stricken child and not just their own.

But somehow, with the odd donation to UNICEF – we

do all seem to be able to switch back to Desperate Housewives. Quality of programming aside, that cannot be right. I found myself, just the other day, devastated by the ongoing carnage in the Middle East. I read all the online op-eds in the Guardian and New York Times, indulged in various unpleasant (for them) fantasies involving George W., his British poodle and a pretzel. About an hour later, emotionally drained, I slumped in front of the television and watched cricket. I really got off my butt and saved the world that evening.

So to summarise (and generalise): mothers have few viable career options when the kids are older; mothers are bored and depressed by this knowledge; mothers can feel their brains rotting as they refuse to buy a Barbie doll for their child at the thousandth time of asking (that afternoon); mothers care about their own *and* other children. And probably, mothers watch too much television.

It's a no-brainer. No, I am not talking about George W. Every mother, everywhere, needs to be working towards a Nobel Prize.

Remember, we mothers at home have a huge advantage over everyone else. Our brains are free. Unless you are working at full capacity waving a rattle in front of a drooling baby – in which case this Guide is not for you – there is a lot of wasted brainpower waiting to be tapped. I get goose bumps just thinking about it.

To be entirely upfront about it, I am not suggesting that you or I will necessarily win a Nobel Prize while still a stay-at-home mum.

I do believe that we should, with a bit of help from this Guide, be laying down the groundwork for that Nobel Prize. Doing this will have a number of distinct advantages. Thinking and planning and taking small steps, individually and with other mums, will keep our brains from atrophying while looking after the kids. Scaling up our efforts will provide us with jobs when the kids are a bit older. *And* a Nobel Prize gives us a long-term career goal.

In addition to this, we will be doing incredibly worthwhile things with our lives and setting a fine example to our children.

Besides, I guarantee that there is nothing we can do in any other career that will match the buzz of making that Nobel acceptance speech someday – with our kids grinning proudly in the first row. So abandon those regrets about the paths not taken and the worries about future forks in the road. You *can* be a stay-at-home mum and have a career, contribute to society and raise children who will do the same.

"You ask, what is our aim? I can answer in one word. It is victory."
(Winston Churchill)

Chapter 2 – Which Nobel?

This is an important question because there are quite a few Nobels – economics, chemistry, physics, medicine, literature and peace. But the thing about this Guide is that it is intended to be an everyman, or to be more precise, everywoman guide. And most of these Nobels are not really within our grasp – be there ever so many guides on how to win one (and as far as I am aware this is the only one).

Medicine, Chemistry and Physics

The days when one could actually win the Science

Nobels (Medicine, Chemistry or Physics) for something that a layman (or laywoman) might *understand*, let alone invent or discover, are long gone. So it is difficult to imagine any of us actually winning one of these Nobels.

Alexander Fleming discovered penicillin by accident. One of his bacterial experiments was contaminated with mould and hey presto! We had antibiotics. I guess most of us could have done that. It is important to say in favour of Fleming that at least he had all that equipment – petri dishes and bacteria and whatnot – hanging around his place so the accident *could* happen. Also, without him, we would all be dead of something that we just pop a few pills for now.

My point is that although we can conceive of discovering penicillin, it is difficult to imagine being involved in "the development of the metathesis method in organic synthesis". I kid you not, that's what the 2005 Nobel Prize for Chemistry was for. And the 2006 Chemistry Prize was awarded to Roger D. Kornberg "for his studies of the molecular basis of eukaryotic transcription." I didn't even understand the 'Chemistry for Idiots' explanation they have on the Nobel website!

Anyway, in the good

be discovered that son

twice. Like Marie Curi

1903 and the Chemistry

radioactivity. Remarkal

the Nobel Prize for Che

as suggested. Othe

.Peace prize as w

And wh

prob

Frankly, the time to aspi

for most of us. There might be a few mothers out there who have the background to win the Medicine, Physics or Chemistry Nobels, in which case I wish you well. But my Guide is intended to help the ordinary become extraordinary – if you are the sort of brain-box who understood what that Chemistry Nobel was about you don't need my help.

Economics

What about the Economics prize? There is a small hope that a stay-at-home mum could win this. But cutting edge economics is all rather mathematics-based at present – statistics and game theory. This last has actually won a Nobel already. The 2005 prize was "for having enhanced our understanding of conflict and cooperation through game-theory analysis". I suspect we haven't quite understood 'conflict and cooperation' as much

wise, this guy would have won the
ell.

at if you really solve one of the big economic
lems of our time, like how to feed all the poor
people in the world by juggling with the numbers? Well,
that would be more of a miracle than feeding the five
thousand and also deserve a Nobel for Peace and not just
Economics.

If you are very good at maths and statistics, I guess you
could go for the Economics Nobel even while at home.
If you keep abreast with current research on the Internet
and keep your brain ticking over weighing up your point
of entry into the debate – the Economics prize is possible.
Not for me because I am hopeless with numbers. I can
only deal in big picture numbers like "a lot" of stay-at-
home mums and "a lot" of mothers trying to win a Nobel
Prize.

Literature

The Literature Nobel is actually a strong outside bet. We
can all write. We might not all write well. I am sure that
there are a few of you out there who are already striking
off the Literature Prize from my list of possibilities

based on the writing in this Guide. But at least we have the basic building blocks from which to construct a book. Whether producing that book means that any of us deserve to be elevated to Nobel Prize winner is a separate story.

My problem with the Literature Prize is that, if you are leading an ordinary family life – husband, two kids or thereabouts, minor but not debilitating financial worries, reasonably distant from any war zone, then, unless you have a really fertile imagination, there just isn't enough experience there to give the book sufficient texture to win the Nobel for Literature.

I vaguely remember that I had a fairly eventful university life. But fifteen years and two kids later, I've actually forgotten the details. Other mothers, whom I hope are the ones reading this Guide, will understand what I mean. My memory is like the leaf from *The Hungry Caterpillar* – full of holes. I have only the most rudimentary grasp of my personal history – and none of the colours and textures. My past is like a dull black and white film. And my present is like the lonely cinemagoer at the afternoon matinee of that film – munching popcorn and wondering why I bothered to turn up.

I do realise that every book is not a disguised autobiography. But when life is a collection of the mundane, it is difficult to imagine being able to write convincingly of strong emotion or with authority on extraneous subjects.

I could be wrong about this.

Being a mother unleashes profoundly primal instincts. Only a mother knows the absolute terror of a child late home from school. Or the overwhelming sorrow and impotence at the sight of a small body in a war zone. We know that our conventional behaviour only disguises the basic instinct to defend our young against anyone using any weapons. In other words, we can switch from living an HBO life to Animal Planet in an instant.

But on balance, I fear that the daily routine of mummy-taxi and homework, dirty dishes and dirty clothes, birthday parties and tuition lessons make it very difficult for a stay-at-home mum to aspire to the Literature Nobel.

I do have a second string to my bow and so can you. If, after the next thirty years spent trying, I do not land one of the other Nobel Prizes, I am hoping that the *attempt* to do so might be worth recording in a book – and give me a real stab at the Literature Prize.

Think ahead, think big and have options!

"Peace, in the sense of the absence of war, is of little value to someone who is dying of hunger or cold. It will not remove the pain of torture inflicted on a prisoner of conscience. It does not comfort those who have lost their loved ones in floods caused by senseless deforestation in a neighboring country. Peace can only last where human rights are respected, where the people are fed, and where individuals and nations are free."
(Dalai Lama)

Chapter 3 – Peace

It has to be Peace. And as a mother – there is no other Nobel Prize that could possibly be more meaningful. But how is a stay-at-home mum going to bring peace? Which war are we going to stop? Do not despair. The roads to peace are many and varied and sufficiently rarely travelled as to give any committed stay-at-home mum a real chance.

The starting point in our quest for the Nobel Peace Prize is to analyse previous winners. It seems from my research that Peace Prize recipients largely fall into a few broad categories – some of which lend themselves to a mother's efforts more naturally than others.

Organisations

Many organisations have won the Nobel Peace Prize including the International Committee of the Red Cross, Amnesty International, the International Campaign to Ban Landmines and Médicins Sans Frontiéres. Occasionally, the founders of these organisations have been awarded a share of the prize, like Jody Williams – the driving force behind the landmines campaign. Others, like Peter Benenson, the founder of Amnesty International (who had his epiphany to start a campaign for prisoners all over the world whilst on a train), did not get a part of the Prize. But he certainly deserved and got his share of the glory.

Two points stand out. Firstly, that Peace is interpreted broadly. Any outfit that protects or serves either people, in the practical physical sense, or fights for their rights (especially within the context of war or state-sponsored unfairness) has a chance. Secondly, any stay-at-home mum, with so much practical experience of need, so much empathy with suffering (and so much control of the family disposable income) – has to be in a great position to see a need and develop the organisation to combat it.

In fact, many of the greatest mass movements in history have been triggered by an individual or a small group. Just remember Gandhi's salt march or the suffragette movement if you do not believe me. The only leverage a mother needs to change the world is a very long plank of an idea to balance on the fulcrum of her back.

Warmongers

If you are in a position to influence a conflict and are willing, whether for reasons of *realpolitik* or conscience, to stop the killing at least temporarily (together with the other party to the war) you are a shoo-in. The road to a Peace Prize is often built on a foundation of corpses. Just think about all those podium moments – Begin/Sadat, Arafat/Rabin-Peres, Hume/Trimble and Kissinger/Le Duc Tho. Personally, I think these guys should have to return the Nobel (unless, like Mr. Le Duc Tho, they turned it down in the first place) if the shooting starts within fifteen minutes of the photoshoot.

I do not think this 'swords into ploughshares' route is one that any self-respecting mother should take. It is really not a big surprise that there are no women in this category of Peace Prize winners.

Greatness Thrust Upon Them

These Prizes are given to people who, by an accident of birth or timing, find themselves in a position where greatness is thrust upon them. They have shouldered a heavy burden – and with it upheld the conscience of every man and woman.

Who are they?

Nelson Mandela, Aung San Suu Kyi, Lech Walesa, Elie Wiesel, Desmond Tutu and Martin Luther King to name a few. It is beyond my ability to write a Guide about becoming like these men or women. It would be an insult to them to try. Keen as I am on my Nobel Prize, the reality of the continuous living martyrdom of Aung San Suu Kyi – under house arrest in Burma, unable to see her children, denied the chance to be at her husband's side when he succumbed to cancer – is enough to force a step back from the precipice.

What these Peace Prize winners have in common is a profound generosity of spirit. They transcend the love of the personal – my children, my family – into a willingness to sacrifice for the wellbeing of all – the children and families of those around me who deserve better.

As a mother, I know, almost without doubt, that I have a 'facing down the tanks in Tianamen Square' moment in me – *if* my children are sheltering behind me. But to protect an ideal? A vision of the future, however appealing? I don't think so. I would like to be wrong about this. But I don't think I am. And I certainly hope never to be put to the test.

To cut to the chase, bearing in mind this is a Guide and therefore an exercise in the art of the possible, I would not choose this road to the Prize for any of us mothers. However, if any of you find yourselves in circumstances where greatness *is* thrust upon you, and it turns out your shoulders are broad enough – or more accurately, your arms are wide enough – for the task, you will certainly deserve your eventual Nobel.

Men in Suits – Ex-Presidents of the United States or Secretary Generals of the United Nations

Only three Presidents of the United States, Theodore Roosevelt, Woodrow Wilson and Jimmy Carter, have won the Nobel Prize. And only two Secretaries General of the United Nations; Dag Hammerskjöld and Kofi Annan. These numbers are quite an indictment of *power*. Rather more than five Nobel Peace Prizes have been awarded since the first one in 1901. It seems that power and influence are rarely a source of peace or good.

Of the three Presidents, Jimmy Carter is the only one who won it largely for work done outside and after high office. That is not surprising as he was viewed as sadly ineffectual in office although I do think history will be kinder to his presidential legacy.

He won it, according to the Nobel Foundation, *"for his decades of untiring effort to find peaceful solutions to international conflicts, to advance democracy and human rights, and to promote economic and social development"*.

This ex-President thing might be a growing category. Bill Clinton must be a good bet for the Peace Prize at some stage with his Clinton Global Initiative on just about everything.

Note to George W. – I realise that you will need thirty years just to memorise your acceptance speech but I really wouldn't bother dusting off the dinner jacket just yet.

Just so George W. does not feel aggrieved at being identified as the last man alive likely to win a Nobel Peace Prize (and invade my neighbourhood in a fit of pique), I am thinking of starting the UnNobel Awards for Incalculable Damage to the Human Race – and George W. is pretty much the only nominee. His prize: Extraordinary Rendition to the dungeons of an Ally in the War on Terror followed by a stint in the care of the US Army in Abu Ghraib and then perhaps permanent retirement to Guantanamo. No torture though, just 'robust interrogation methods'.

Anyway, back to the Guide. Unless they change the rules for Arnie 'the Terminator' turned 'Governator', and this is unlikely as he has turned out to be a liberal 'girlie man' under the muscle bound exterior (worried about climate change, what next?), you have to be a US citizen (and born in the US as well) to be President of the United States. As for the top UN job, you probably need to speak French – or there is always a real chance that France, as a member of the Security Council, might veto your nomination.

Assuming that you fit into either of these categories – I am pretty sure there is no such thing as a US citizen who speaks French – then bear in mind that all your good works as US President or UN Secretary General might land you a Nobel Peace Prize as well. But let's face it – the average stay-at-mum is not just a US Passport or French lesson away from either of those jobs!

Religious Types

Probably only the 14th Dalai Lama and Mother Theresa fall squarely into this category. I have to say I am not that comfortable with Nobel Prizes going to religious types (and apparently the Nobel Committee isn't that keen either!). Religion is such a profoundly divisive subject (notwithstanding what its proponents' claim) that it has no place in a conversation about Peace.

To give them their due, I doubt that either the Dalai Lama, as an advocate of Tibetan freedom, or Mother Theresa, as a champion of the downtrodden – would have acted that differently without their religious underpinning. Anyway, I refuse to hand out any guidance on a religious path to the Nobel. If God is behind your good works (or bad) then I am sure you can wait for your reward in heaven rather than competing with the rest of us whose immortality depends on human memory.

Our Best Chance

Only 33 of the 784 previous Nobel Prize winners have been women. Twelve of these 33 women won the Nobel Peace Prize. At first glance, the odds do seem stacked against us mothers. But in the last 30 years (since 1976), there have been *nine* female Nobel Peace Prize winners. In other words, our chances have improved dramatically, to almost one in three. Why is this?

The usual social advancement arguments apply – more women are educated, have jobs, are in positions of influence than ever before – by definition women should be improving their collection of Prizes.

But for me, the main reason that there are more women reaching the podium is the nature of the issues that are confronting our generation and the expanding definition of peace. This gives me hope that any woman, but especially a stay-at-home mum, has a better chance than most at winning a Nobel Peace Prize.

Take Wangari Maathai, the most recent female winner and a mother of three, who won *"for her contribution to sustainable development, democracy and peace"*. The Presentation Speech by the Chairman of the Norwegian Nobel Committee to Wangari Maathai made it clear that the Nobel Committee was intentionally broadening the definition of Peace to take into account the twenty-first century problems faced by the human race. To quote the speech:

> *"The Norwegian Nobel Committee has for a long time maintained that there are many different paths to peace. The Committee's Peace concept is in other words a broad one. This explains why many different categories of persons and organizations have received the Nobel Peace Prize. Statesmen and politicians can contribute at the international, the regional and the national level, and many have been awarded the prize. Major humanitarian organizations, and individuals engaged in humanitarian work, have also been recognized. Humanitarian work must in the highest degree be seen as promoting the "fraternity between nations" of which Alfred Nobel speaks in*

his will. The many awards to those who have worked for disarmament or arms control relate directly to the "abolition or reduction of standing armies" that Nobel also mentions. In recent decades, the Nobel Committee has made human rights a central element of the definition of peace. There were many warnings against such a broadening of the concept of peace. Today there are few things peace researchers and other scholars are readier to agree on than precisely that democracy and human rights advance peace."

In an almost embarrassed way, the Chairman goes on to ask, "But where does tree-planting come in?"

Wangari Maathai was the perfect example of a new type of winner because she covered both the older understanding of peace, by standing up to Daniel Arap Moi, the Kenyan despot, and being imprisoned and vilified for her efforts – AND she planted trees! The Nobel Committee could have ignored her latter efforts and rewarded her for her traditional battles on behalf of Kenyan women and against oppressive regimes. But it intentionally added a discussion of her tree planting efforts, albeit in a rather convoluted 'men in suits coming to terms with tree huggers' kind of way.

The Chairman expanded the discussion as follows:

"When we analyze local conflicts, we tend to focus on their ethnic and religious aspects. But it is often the underlying ecological circumstances that bring the more readily visible factors to the flashpoint. Consider the conflict in Darfur in the Sudan. What catches the eye is that this is a conflict between Arabs and Africans, between the government, various armed militia groups, and civilians. Below this surface, however, lies the desertification that has taken place in the last few decades, especially in northern Darfur. The desert has spread southwards, forcing Arab nomads further and further south year-by-year, bringing them into conflict with African farmers. In the Philippines, uncontrolled deforestation has helped to provoke a rising against the authorities. In Mexico, soil erosion and deforestation have been factors in the revolt in Chiapas against the central government. In Haiti, in Amazonas, and in the Himalayas, deforestation and the resulting soil erosion have contributed to deteriorating living conditions and caused tension between population groups and countries. In many countries deforestation, often together with other problems, leads to migration to the big cities, where

the lack of infrastructure is another source of further conflict.

Can all this not be said more simply? Maathai herself has put it like this: "We are sharing our resources in a very inequitable way. We have parts of the world that are very deprived and parts of the world that are very rich. And that is partly the reason why we have conflicts." Wars and conflicts certainly have many other causes, too. But who would deny that inequitable distribution, locally and internationally, is relevant in this connection? I predict that within a few decades, when researchers have developed more comprehensive analyses of many of the world's conflicts, the relation between the environment, resources and conflict may seem almost as obvious as the connection we see today between human rights, democracy and peace.

Another thing that needs to be said in this context is that sooner or later, in order to meet environmental problems, there will have to be international cooperation across all national boundaries on a much larger scale than we have seen up to now. We live on the same globe. We must all cooperate to meet the world's environmental challenges. Together we are strong, divided we are weak."

33

I would add that handing out Peace Prizes for individual dispute resolution in this time of violent climate change, depleting natural resources and global confrontation will have that nasty "fiddling while Rome burns" (or strumming while New Orleans drowns) kind of feel to it.

It does seem that, as the Nobel Committee widens its definition of peace, it is becoming more relevant to the issues that face all mothers everywhere. A concomitant of this is that as we mothers confront the issues that will affect the very future of our children, which are the same issues that might now lead to that Holy Grail of high effort and purpose, the Nobel Peace Prize - we might actually win one!

I know there are a few of you mothers out there thinking that making the world safe for our children should be reward enough. In a sense I agree, but a little bit of recognition goes a long way. Besides, it gives our efforts to achieve 'peace' in its various guises, a single dominant purpose. *And* it gives us that critical career goal to motivate us on those days when saving the world does seem awfully hard work. And if mothers are, as a matter of practice trying for the Nobel Peace Prize, it will undoubtedly inspire the next generation of women and mothers confronting the usual motherhood versus work dilemma.

Also, we have to assume this is an ongoing process. Even at my most optimistic, I cannot see that every major problem confronting humanity will have been successfully resolved in the next thirty years, regardless of how many mothers are addressing their minds to the issue. A Nobel Peace Prize brings much needed publicity and cash to individual hard work. The resulting publicity might actually *elevate* those efforts into the global phenomenon the recipient was trying to achieve in the first place.

"I have nothing to offer but blood, toil, tears and sweat."
(Winston Churchill)

Chapter 4 – Frontrunners

Before I get into suggestion mode for issues that a mother could address to win a Nobel Peace Prize, I want to go through a brief and random list of frontrunners. This is not intended to discourage you – in my estimation these people will be getting theirs within the next ten to twenty years and we are looking at thirty years at least before the mothers' Nobel generation reaches its peak.

Not surprisingly, as they spend less time at home bringing up the children, the men in suits are still at the top of the charts. Note to George W. – I don't mean you.

Bill Clinton

Bill made his first big push for the Nobel Peace Prize by actually striving for Middle East Peace.

Not that long ago, George W. was looking for a "sustainable peace" between Israel and Hizbullah. This apparently required one of the two possible parties to any future peace agreement to be completely wiped out. In a sense, it would have obviated the possibility of war or the need for peace. I don't have the current President's ear, although I do have this vision of an aide whispering some advice in his right ear, and his words being clearly audible to others as it comes out the left. However, I would appreciate it if someone would explain to George W. that, by his definition, the various genocides we have witnessed in the all too recent past: Germany, Rwanda, Yugoslavia, Sudan, actually involve one side looking for a "sustainable peace".

George W.'s shortcomings do shine a spotlight on Clinton's statesman-like attempt to find a just peace in the Middle East. Sadly, as he failed and his successor has engulfed the Middle East in flames, Bill is not going to win it for having come closer than most.

He should not despair though. His Clinton Global Initiative, harnessing big business and big thinkers to solve pressing Third World problems, is precisely the sort of thing the Nobel Committee likes – just look at the Carter Center.

To quote its website:

> *"The Clinton Global Initiative is a non-partisan catalyst for action, bringing together a community of global leaders to devise and implement innovative solutions to some of the world's most pressing challenges."*

It may sound like the brochure for an MBA course, but in a sense it is precisely what we should all be trying, albeit with a less comprehensive Rolodex. All Bill is doing is using his contacts to take active steps towards measurable goals. We can all do that. On a lesser scale to begin with but we have two advantages. There are more mothers than ex-Presidents of the United States (even if you count the nasty ones) and we are younger.

The Clinton Global Initiative, his occasional forays into tsunami zones and an understandable wistfulness for the good old days before George W., make Bill a very safe bet for a Nobel Peace Prize at some stage. All he has to do is actually produce some measurable results and maintain the effort for ten years.

Bill Gates

Bill Gates is the founder of Microsoft, the richest man in the world and a philanthropist. I suspect that there are only two possible reasons that Bill (and probably, Melinda Gates too) hasn't won it yet. The Nobel Committee is suspicious of new wealth and computers (the two together must be an anathema) or they are reluctant to interrupt his good works for long enough to drag him up to Norway. Actually, I bet the real reason is that he is still too involved with Microsoft. The minute he steps down from having an active management role, Bill Gates will get his Peace Prize. And it will probably be sooner rather than later, with the Buffet fortune to utilise as well.

As set out on the website of the Gates Foundation:

> *"Guided by the belief that every life has equal value, the Bill & Melinda Gates Foundation works to reduce inequities and improve lives around the world."*

It may sound trite. He is, after all, a nerdy computer geek with a bad haircut. But the Gates Foundation is tackling the big issues head on. As and when Bill Gates gets his Nobel, it will be well-deserved.

Bob Geldof and Bono

I am not sure about these two. I suspect the Nobel Committee will be hesitant to give the prize to anyone who was a celebrity first and an activist second. Having said that, in this age where politics is dead and politicians ought to be, only celebrities have the capacity to reach out to the citizenry. It may not be an attractive development but it is the reality we live with. Celebrities can achieve a huge amount when it comes to raising awareness of global issues.

And from Live Aid to Live 8, Bob and Bono have done more to raise awareness and money for global poverty than many of the best-intentioned politicians (if that is not an oxymoron). Their celebrity gives them important assets – a following, money, access to today's politicians (who are always desperate for a bit of reflected glory) and media coverage. If the celebrity has the brains and the energy to channel this for good – perhaps he/ she should not be excluded from consideration by our cynicism about the celebrity endorsement.

The key here is that the celebrity should have to put in a lot of running before he is even considered for a Nobel. In other words, Bono, Bob – I think you should get your Nobels some day. Let's just hope that twenty years from now – Live Something Else is unnecessary.

Other possibilities

I have a soft spot for a few women who must have an outside chance – especially if they keep at it for a while. They are all intelligent and principled – some are beautiful as well. I have to confess that if they top off these accomplishments with a Nobel Peace Prize, I will have to work quite hard not to come over just a tiny bit bitchy.

Helena Kennedy

Helena Kennedy consistently speaks out against the undermining of civil liberties by the war on terror. People like her have been a bulwark against populist, reactionary legislating by a United Kingdom Parliament cowed by their participation in the foreign policy disasters of this era and clinging to the hope of continued office by the adoption of tabloid-driven short-term agendas. She is also Queen's Counsel (a very senior barrister) and has been made a life peer in the House of Lords. To me, her willingness to speak out for her beliefs despite being ostensibly a member of the establishment sets her apart from the rest.

Arundhati Roy

Her first novel, The God of Small Things, won the Booker Prize and was described in the New York Review of Books as *"so morally strenuous and so imaginatively supple that the reader remains enthralled all the way through"*. Instead of cashing in on her success by writing a second novel, she has instead become a social activist who is using her moral authority to speak out – targeting everything from environmental degradation (the Narmada Dam project in India) to the nuclear weapons race on the Indian sub-continent. For her pains, she has been sued, vilified as anti-Indian and anti-American and become the poster child of the anti-globalisation movement. Arundhati Roy uses her enormous talent with words to drag our attention to the things we would rather walk away from and forget.

Anita Roddick

Anita Roddick's achievement is not to have confronted the forces of capitalism but to have harnessed them. Her brainchild, The Body Shop, despite being sold recently to L'Oreal, is still a global franchise which operates along ethical lines including supporting community trade, promoting environmental sustainability, rejecting animal testing and supporting human rights initiatives. And she is not resting on her laurels but continues to use her success and stature to campaign for other global causes she feels passionately about.

Stay-at-Home Mums

So now we know the sort of competition we might face to win a Nobel Peace Prize. But what must each of us do to join such exalted company?

I believe that we need to extrapolate from our own personal experiences as mothers. What is it that we cannot stand by and watch? What do we believe is the single greatest threat to our children's present and future wellbeing?

Child labour? Because we can imagine our children on the tea plantations and in the sweatshops?

Women's rights? Because we cannot imagine being denied the vote we have no time to cast?

Drugs? Because we are terrified that illegal drugs and the violence associated with it might touch our families?

There is almost no end to the issues that a mother might feel passionately about.

The purpose of this Guide is to demonstrate that you can choose an issue, research it thoroughly, determine what best you can do to confront that issue and extrapolate a template for social change. The next step is to work towards that goal with a small group of like-minded people, eventually scaling up your efforts to change the world for the better.

Mothers are spoilt for choice when it comes to issues we could address in pursuit of our respective Nobel Prizes. It is just as well we are a large group. As individuals, therefore, we probably don't need to come up with more than a couple of good ideas each to make a difference. Next stop after that is Norway!

"The future ain't what it used to be."
(Yogi Berra)

Chapter 5 – Spoilt for Choice – Climate Change

You don't need to be a scientist to know that the weather is changing. Any idiot (except the one in the White House) can see that it is getting hotter and we might all die as a result of extreme weather conditions.

There are big examples: the ice caps are melting, sea levels are rising, storms are devastating, deserts are expanding, acid rain is prevalent, coral reefs are bleaching and dying, and small examples: every other day is a 'new record since records were kept' – heat wave in Europe, cold snap in South Africa, heat wave in California, cold snap in New York. Let's face it, like it or not, the weather is not the same as when we were young. It *has* changed.

In addition, we are not all that far away from a major calamity.

We know that trapped methane gas from the frozen bogs of Siberia might start seeping into the atmosphere at a great rate if its ice covering melts. This will increase the warming effect dramatically.

We know that if the seas keep getting warmer a shutdown or slowdown of the ocean currents (including the Gulf Stream that moderates temperatures in northern Europe) is a distinct possibility, leading to irreversible climatic change.

We know that a substantial number of species are critically endangered or endangered. Polar bears are actually *drowning* because they can't find the next patch of ice.

We know that the Greenland and West Antartica ice sheets might increase their rate of melting suddenly – increasing sea levels much more quickly than currently anticipated.

If you don't believe this accelerated melting is likely, think about what it's like when the ice cubes in your gin and tonic start melting – first you have those pristine frozen cubes, then the cubes start getting rounded at the edges. The next thing you know, your drink is too watery and you have to top up the gin. In my case, as every watery drink reminds me of the horrors of impending climate change, I top up the gin with a liberal hand.

There is also no doubt about the primary cause of the problem – greenhouse gas emissions plus hot air from the White House. Forget all the politicians and scientists who tell you otherwise. They are either in hock to vested interests or thick (George W. is both). Especially ignore all those people who will tell you that the US/global/ Kazakh economy will come to a grinding halt if you try and address climate change. Sure, the car companies might go bust, but the bike companies will thrive. Oil companies might suffer, but wind farm profits will blow their shareholders away.

In any event, any argument that suggests we should continue to do the thing that will *kill* us (and our families) because stopping might cost us money is ridiculous.

Also, ignore all the people who argue that progress is inevitable and we, the human race who created the problem, will find a way to fix it. It is not entirely impossible, I suppose. But is it a risk we are prepared to take? Stop reading this for a second and go and have a peek at one of your children. Is he sleeping? Curled up with his grubby teddy bear, tousled head on his pillow, blankets on the floor. Are you really going to trust his future to the possibility that some boffin somewhere might find a 'solution' to global warming?

Many of the mothers I know are panic stricken about climate change and religious about recycling and switching off the air-conditioning/heating, but then pack their bags and fly the whole family to sunny somewhere on a low cost airline. It just won't do.

I've even overheard conversations about property purchases that try to take into account possible weather pattern changes. It goes something like this, "We were going to buy a holiday place on the Mediterranean, but prices are so high at the moment. In the end we opted for Scotland. The land was dirt cheap – and in about twenty years it will be breezy and balmy." Even if this was true, and I fear theirs was an inexact guess about an inexact science, will you feel quite so happy in your holiday villa while Grandpa and Grandma are drowning in London?

And don't be under any illusions. Global warming is your fault. And mine. The rest of the six billion people barely get a look in. The people who are scratching out a living on some Ethiopian coffee plantation, Chinese rice field or Indian cotton farm are not the problem.

Greenhouse gases are emitted into the atmosphere when we burn fossil fuels to generate electricity or heat (that's the hot water, lights, heating or air-conditioning, fridge, washing machine and television) or to power engines for travel (that's the car – and the plane for the holiday as well). These gases trap some of the sun's energy within our atmosphere – like a greenhouse roof – increasing the Earth's temperature. The main greenhouse gas is carbon dioxide (CO_2). This accounts for about two thirds of the human-induced warming effect.

It is somewhat ironic that just about everything we do is eventually going to ruin the planet. This is also what makes it so hard to deal with, for us as individuals, as well as for our elected leaders who fear that reducing our consumer lifestyle choices might be a shortcut to early retirement. It takes more will power than most people have, including myself, to switch off the air-conditioning, walk to the shops, make sure no electrical device is left on 'standby' at night and drop the long distance holiday.

I do sometimes feel, when I read the news on climate change, that the only solution is for my family and I to huddle in the middle of a field somewhere – trying to take as shallow breaths as possible.

If this appears to be the best guess at the lifestyle change required to combat climate change – it is no wonder that we go ahead and book that eco-holiday(!) to somewhere far away. If we're going to die, we might as well have lived life to the fullest – as defined by consumer lifestyle magazines.

But this is where the Nobel Peace Prize comes in. By focusing on steps that you can take *personally*, you can really make a difference. And previously, it might have seemed like a haphazard, desultory effort (in effect, a game of 'whack a mole') – with no measurable goals. Now you know that what you are doing is experimenting with different methods of saving the planet. If your plan happens to be the one that works and catches on, first with other mothers and then with everyone – the Peace Prize is yours.

What we can do as Individuals

Clearly, we have to change our lifestyles first. But rather than be constantly undermining our own efforts with the 'one step forward followed by a holiday by plane in the opposite direction' approach to lifestyle change – I think it would be much more measurable to aim for *carbon neutral* lifestyles. That means reducing our personal carbon footprint as far as possible (i.e. take the bus, carpool, ride a bike to the shops, turn out the lights and never leave anything electrical on standby mode). But we also need to compensate for the moments of weakness, as well as all the other moments of necessity, by adopting offsetting strategies.

The great thing is that working out what to do to offset carbon emissions has never been easier – a bit of research on the Internet offers every alternative from tree planting to investing in wind farms. Just look at www.nobelmums.com for a few examples. This is a website I have set up to try and share information on what we mothers can do about the issues raised in this Guide.

I have often heard people bring up the old enforcement question – how do we know they are really planting trees when we pay someone over the Internet to do it? It is important to choose an organisation with a track record, a transparent audit trail, preferably endorsed by a reputable NGO, charity or government. At the end of the day, the more people that sign up for these carbon neutral programmes, the greater the scrutiny there will be. In the meantime, refusing to take part because of concerns about veracity is like refusing to go to the doctor in case he slips you a placebo – a plain dumb attitude that is probably going to kill you.

The other amazing thing, from my research so far, is that eliminating a family's carbon footprint for a year does not cost as much as you might imagine. We are still talking about giving up the odd shopping trip – not handing over our firstborn. If you don't believe me, look at www.nobelmums.com!

Scaling Up

This is all very well and good of course – but nobody is ever going to win a Nobel by buying carbon emission rights for their family holiday. The key is to *scale-up*. And this is where mothers have a huge advantage over everyone else. We mothers are a vast network of like-minded people concerned about the future of our children. It will never be easier to have the conversation. And it is in the scaling up that the Nobel comes into play. We need to come up with a simple scheme that persuades people to adopt carbon neutral lives – by reducing their carbon footprints and offsetting the rest. If it works, we will have a simple template that can be used by other groups of mothers and eventually society generally to address climate change.

The key is not to panic by thinking globally and deciding the problem is too big and therefore it has to be someone else's to fix. Start small. Try and first persuade family and friends to take up the scheme you come up with and if it works, roll it out slowly to others. That's how it starts – fast forward thirty years and you will be making your Nobel acceptance speech. That is pretty much how Wangari Maathai got her Nobel after all.

If your scheme doesn't work – too dull, too hard, too preachy – tweak it and try again. We have all the years when at home with the kids to practice on family, friends and fellow mothers. Once a template is identified that works – you will be ready to take it on the road as the kids grow older.

What works will depend on the type of society you live in and the sort of person you are. But here are a few ideas:

- get together with a few friends, work out your household carbon emissions (you just need your electricity bill, car make and model, fuel consumption and miles travelled in a given period and an estimate of your holiday travel – average out the last few years). Get everyone to sign up to a carbon neutral plan. If this works, start rolling it out to other friends and nag the husband to bring it up at work.

  You can inject a bit of fun and keep people interested if you choose interesting offsetting ways. Wangari Maathai planted trees all over Kenya. You could, together with other mothers, green the neighbourhood, the school, the road to work, a small neighbouring country – whatever catches your fancy. The important thing is to select achievable bite-sized goals.

- Alternatively, have a competition. Get a group of mums involved. Put some money into a pot – whoever reduces their carbon footprint the maximum in a given period (as measured by electricity bills or such like) sweeps the lot! The next step might be to get local government or a company to sponsor the prize and widen the competition. Do avoid asking a car company for some gas-guzzling SUV.

We should also lobby government. Once mothers have made it clear to our dear leaders that they can only have our votes if they stop trying to micromanage our lives and focus on macro-managing the environment instead – something might actually get done. Lobby them to put up fuel prices – but make it clear we want to see the extra tax money go directly into green public transportation. Lobby for windfall profits on oil companies. Again, warn our leaders that we need to see the money used for green research. Substantially reduce the tax on hybrid/ electric cars to make them affordable. And of course, ban Chelsea tractors.

Can you believe the irony? Governments are finally cracking down on cigarettes in public spaces to protect us from passive smoking. Great – now we can step outside and take a deep, health-giving breath of exhaust fumes and factory smoke.

These ideas may seem ordinary and I would be delighted if you or some other mother produced something better. The whole point is to tap the under-utilised imaginations of mothers at home and use our daily experiences to confront the problems of our time. I put out these ideas merely to suggest that coming up with something *is* possible.

Not every single idea a mother comes up with is going to be practical or scaleable. But if we are all trying to come up with the Nobel-winning idea, first and foremost, our *own* impact on the environment will be minimised.

And with all of us mothers using our under-utilised brainpower to find a way to encourage carbon neutrality on the part of others, one of us is bound to succeed. And if your idea is the planet-saving one, then the Nobel Peace Prize will be yours one day!

"Whoever said money can't buy happiness simply didn't know where to go shopping."
(Bo Derek)

Chapter 6–Spoilt for Choice–Ethical Consumerism

The bad news is that your carbon emissions (and mine) are not the sum of our damage to the planet. The usual carbon monitors measure what we *use*. These monitors *do not* measure the emissions we generate in others. This might not seem, at first glance, to make sense. You didn't beg the neighbour to go on holiday or to leave the lights on while they were away. I certainly didn't ask mine to buy an SUV.

Think about it this way. Within the space of this last week – did one of your children throw a tantrum in a supermarket? And did you buy them the cheapest plastic toy you could find to shut them up? By doing that, you might have encouraged a rainforest-burning, greenhouse gas-emitting, sweatshop labour-using plastic toy factory, tucked somewhere out of sight and out of mind, to keep manufacturing more of those toys that don't last the car trip home.

If we generate the demand, someone will fulfill it. We are consumers. And because in this modern era we do not see where the goods are coming from or how they are being produced, it is very difficult to be sure that they have been produced in an environmentally sound and ethical way. In fact, if anything – we can be sure they were not.

Which brings us neatly to the next Nobel Prize winning strategy – ethical consumerism.

It is no use saying that we do not know where the stuff we buy comes from. Ours is a greater responsibility than that. By ignoring the origins and composition of what we buy, we are complicit in the exploitation of people (including children) and the planet.

You will, however, be pleased to know that ethical consumerism on a personal level is actually not that difficult to achieve. Further, if more mothers insist on consuming ethically or not at all – production methods will soon improve.

Even better than that, we would have set an example to the burgeoning middle classes in India and China. Instead of aspiring to emulate us by adopting our present methods and volume of consumption, it will be the 'done thing' to buy only ethical products. They can skip the Wal-Mart generation.

Besides, it is the factories in these countries that are churning out the cheap consumables which we buy. Once they (and their owners in the rest of the world) are compelled to adopt environmentally sound production methods in order to sell anything to us at all, there won't be any cheap rubbish left on the shelves.

We are constantly being urged to buy stuff. The ads on TV and in glossy magazines, product placements, radio jingles, pop-up windows on our personal computers, the pictures of celebrities shopping, the free gifts, the 'collectibles' (what a word – it sums up beautifully the pointlessness of most of our shopping), the 'two for one' offers and the discounts. The message, overt and subliminal, is buy, buy, BUY!

If we don't have everything that everyone else has and then some, we perceive ourselves as failures, both as parents and as human beings. Fulfilling this rampant consumerism is destroying our environment. It is no use being carbon neutral at home if your shopping habits are the catalyst for more and more production and destruction.

And we are teaching it to our children too. My children behave as if they have been given a public beating if I refuse to buy them something in a shop – and they are always asking for something that one of their friends has – usually some 'collectible' from MacDonald's or such like. One of the advantages with ethical consumerism on a personal level is that if all mothers do it, we won't ever have to hear about what so and so has!

So, how to go about consuming ethically and how to leverage this into a Nobel Prize?

What we can do as Individuals

Consuming ethically can be divided into two parts – necessities and fluff.

Necessities – Organic and Fairtrade

The things we need to buy, we need to buy sensibly. Organic as much as possible, Fairtrade at every opportunity. This can be expensive. But it is important to remember that Fairtrade and organic products cost a bit more because these products are trying to accurately reflect the costs of production. In other words, it is not that these goods are too expensive – it is that the other stuff is too *cheap*. Too cheap because they use exploitative farming methods that adversely affect the land, the consequences of which will eventually be in our streams and bloodstreams. Too cheap because they do not provide the farmers and plantation workers a decent living standard. I am not talking about holidays and a family car by the way – I mean food, shoes and school.

I had an argument with my mother yesterday. She said she loves the idea but she just cannot afford to buy Fairtrade coffee. The bottom line is that if we can't afford to buy goods that meet minimum ethical standards, we cannot afford to buy them *at all*. My mother will have to give up coffee. The planet really cannot afford the hidden cost of our continuing to buy cheap produce.

Please note that when I say we should pay a price that reflects the true costs – I do not mean that we should buy the most expensive product we can find. If it is not clearly labelled as organic or Fairtrade, all you are doing is paying a premium to the coffee company – there is no guarantee that any extra money has trickled down to the farmer or that better farming methods have been used.

Further, although these organic and/or Fairtrade products are a bit more expensive, some of this price differential can be attributed to middlemen inflating prices for consumers with a conscience. The more you use ethical products, the more suppliers will enter the market and pricing will become more competitive (but subject to an ethical 'floor').

The Fairtrade revolution is a good example of this. The Fairtrade label is an independent consumer guarantee, monitored by non-profit organisations, that Third World farmers and plantation workers get a better deal. Although there have been teething problems, the odd scandal and plenty of economists jumping up and down and gnashing their teeth at the idea of the "market" not setting prices for wages/commodities, the reality is that it has lifted thousands of families out of poverty. I expect the Fairtrade-labelling organisations might be in the running for a Nobel for their efforts.

The point to make to these economists is that there *is* demand for non-exploitative products – as the success of the Fairtrade venture shows. Further, any market analysis assumes participants with free will and the ability to walk away from an unfair deal. Not the easiest thing to do when the pittance the coffee farmer is being offered for his crop by some greedy coffee buyer is still the difference between food for his children or the family going to bed hungry. In many instances, the farmer is not in a position to reject a buyer just because he has not covered the costs of production and has no extra funds for new tools, fertilisers or seeds for the next season.

No doubt these economists believe that the farmer scratching out a living in Ethiopia can surf the net, check the current commodity prices, call a purchaser prepared to pay more on his cell phone and fly to London to close the deal. Or alternatively, after a bad year of low prices, perhaps he can diversify his crops or retrain as a computer analyst. His children will be dead by then so he might have some spare cash.

The wonderful thing about Fairtrade or organic purchases is that it helps directly. With a lot of the other stuff – you become carbon neutral and the neighbour buys a four-wheel drive. The effect of your efforts can be negated by others. But if you purchase organic stuff, you know that somewhere there *is* a plantation that is not pumping harmful pesticides onto your food (and into the air and the nearest water supply). And if you buy Fairtrade, extra money *has* gone to the farmer. The neighbour can't pick his pocket.

Ethical food product labelling is now expanding beyond the organic and Fairtrade concepts as well. For instance, the Marine Stewardship Council (MSC) label helps identify fish that have been caught from managed stocks using ethical fishing methods. Various supermarkets all over the world now stock MSC-labelled fish – a small first step towards ensuring the survival of numerous marine species currently threatened. The key, as with the whole movement to ethical consumerism, is that it requires the consumer (i.e. you and me) to cooperate.

Food Miles

I have a friend to whom I mentioned that I had been reading up on "food miles" and it had really opened my eyes to a new issue. She said (she might have been joking), "But I thought you only got air miles if you flew yourself!"

If there is an apple orchard down the road, there is no need to eat imported New Zealand apples. If there is a banana plantation down the road, there is no need to eat imported Florida bananas. This is because of the environmental cost of freight. The more 'food miles' your apples or bananas travelled, the worse it is for the environment. And airfreight is much, much worse than sea freight. For instance, importing 1kg of strawberries by air from California to the United Kingdom is apparently the equivalent of keeping a 100-watt bulb on for eight days!

If the fruits you like are seasonal, do without that fruit the rest of the year. Anticipate spring with pleasure. Don't fly a strawberry from California to the UK to feed your habit. The environmental cost of our desire for seasonal fruits all year round is unacceptable.

If you are from a country that does not grow apples or strawberries, then perhaps you should be developing a taste for papayas and watermelons. Apples and strawberries should be an expensive treat (to reflect the real cost to the environment of getting them to your supermarket)!

Ideally, the additional environmental costs of freight should be compensated for by the freight company adopting carbon neutralising methods and absorbing or passing on that cost. This would make California strawberries more expensive – but again it would only be reflecting the "real cost" of the product. If the strawberries are good enough to be worth flying half way across the world, people will still buy it, even if it is charged in a manner that reflects its frequent flyer points.

If the imported stuff is a 'necessity', like coffee, that is unlikely to be grown down the road and also requires processing, we need to pay a price that reflects its entire production and travel costs. Usually, non-perishable foodstuff is shipped rather than sent by air. This has much less impact on the environment per pound of the product. However, we still have to ensure that our coffee was grown in a manner that is sustainable and that the farmers got a fair deal.

The 'other' necessities

What about the other twenty-first century necessities like the car and the television? I am not going to suggest you give up electrical goods! I am also going to assume (see the previous chapter on global warming) that you are on the road to making your electricity consumption carbon neutral (through reduced use as well as offsetting strategies).

The only step left is to do the research on which type of product to buy by researching the manufacturers' ethics. Basically, this involves reading up on the product, the company and checking the press (especially what consumer and green magazines have to say). Some choices are easy – a hybrid car is better than a petrol car. An electric car, if your use is purely urban, is better than a hybrid. (By the way, please don't rush out and trade-in the car. This discussion is premised on your being about to buy one of these products anyway. A significant amount of the global warming caused by cars is in the manufacturing process.) Buying a hybrid is great not only because of the obvious benefits but also because as consumers we are signalling to car manufacturers that they need to be exploring green technologies for their cars or lose a substantial section of the 'mummy mobile' market.

Remarkably, there is a lot of green stuff out there – everything from light bulbs to energy efficient fridges. We just have to make a conscious effort to do the research before making the choice. And again, there are plenty of green consumer magazines on the Internet with reams of good advice. As an example, I tested this theory by Googling 'energy efficient kitchen appliances guide' and was immediately pointed in the direction of energy and water efficient appliances. And we should not limit our investigation to the 'greenness' of the device. Companies that make an effort to minimise, and then neutralise, the environmental impact of the *production* process, should also be rewarded through our purchases.

And the fantastic thing about energy labelling is that you can adopt the highest standards available across the globe. For instance, if the country where you live does not have standards or they are not very strict – all you have to do is look on the Internet for countries with better labelling requirements, identify the best model of fridge or washing machine and then demand the same make and model at the local shop. It might not have the right sticker but you have researched the best buy in the most intelligent way for the future of the planet.

Finally, when you buy one of these appliances, tell the shop that your choice was based on the green credentials of the device or the company. A few million mums walk in and make that point and we will revolutionise the design of every fridge, television and dishwasher on the planet.

The Stuff you don't Need

Here's an idea about the stuff you don't need – *don't* buy it. I am currently proving that this is possible by not buying anything other than food this month. This is not a permanent solution but I thought going cold turkey might help make it easier to shop less in the coming months. I have also made a promise to myself that I will only buy ethical gifts for Christmas. In fact, I just discovered you can plant a tree for someone at Christmas!

As a citizen in a democracy, I am always struck by how useless my vote is. I have voted since coming of age almost without fail in a constituency that has elected the other candidate by significant majorities each time.

The United Kingdom is a good example of the failures of democracy. (I exclude the US as an example because the 2000 presidential election was not a failure so much as a farce.) One presumably cannot ever vote for Tony Blair again because poodles should not hold high office. His successors are tainted with his mistakes. You could vote for the Liberal Democrats, but apparently the only thing they *could* organise is a piss-up in a brewery. And that leaves the Tories – great. I personally will *never* trust a politician with big hair again.

In any event, that precious vote, available once every four to five years is a very blunt instrument. It is entirely possible that you or I might support some part of a party's platform but are strongly opposed to others.

In that sense, our dollar is a much more powerful weapon than our vote. We can decide exactly how to spend it. And whatever we decide to spend it on has consequences. If we purchase over-packaged, unsustainable rubbish – more of it is generated. We have by that powerful act of spending, created a market. If others have the same penchant for over-packaged unsustainable rubbish – other suppliers will soon be jumping on the bandwagon, cutting down swathes of forest, building colossal fume-spewing factories and paying their workers a pittance.

We read in the papers about exploitative employers, child workers or another rainforest cut down, and shake our heads and get all indignant. We angrily demand to know why they don't have laws to stop this sort of thing from happening. The only way to enforce such a law would be to throw us all in jail and then throw away the key. Really. We created the problem. You and I and our cheap clothes and cheap toys.

If, however, instead of wielding our purses for evil, we were a force for good – the knock on effects would be visible very quickly. Let's say for the sake of argument that as consumers we rejected anything and everything that was not ethically produced – in a very short while the business environment would change and so would the global environment.

It goes without saying that nothing in this new ideal world is going to be that cheap. We will all be buying less of everything and paying more for it. But we would have abandoned planet-destroying over-consumption. The term 'collectible' will appear only in the fuller dictionaries with 'archaic' next to it. Don't you think a world in which we all have less stuff, but what we have is high quality, beautiful and long-lasting, would be a better one?

Every time you spend a dollar, remember that it is *your vote* in our collective consumer democracy. Think about it. Would any of us vote for a politician who promised us more pollution, more exploitation of the poor and a bleak future for the planet and our children? No? Then why are we voting for those outcomes with our money?

If we *are* going to buy something – we need to make a real effort to read the labels. Many books are printed on recycled or sustainable forest paper (for instance, Al Gore's An Inconvenient Truth) – others aren't. Wooden toys are made of sustainable forest wood – or they are not. If they are not, or we can't tell from the packaging, we should just not buy it. As beautiful or educational as the toy seems to be, just think for a moment how beautiful that tree would have been, standing tall in some forest somewhere.

Most toys are overpackaged – the box, the clear plastic, the cardboard packing material, the wires to hold it down, the batteries, the plastic bag to bring it home in – and this before the impact of the plastic toy itself – its manufacture, use and eventual place in a landfill. Did we *really* have to buy that toy? I am sure we could have found a delightful handmade stuffed animal made by a women's co-operative in Sri Lanka and carried it home in our handbags.

And anyway, your children (and mine) really *can* wear hand me downs and play with old toys. They do not need brand new mock kitchen sets, doctors' kits, dollhouses, toolboxes, musical instruments, every single superhero outfit and fairy dresses in seventeen shades of pink.

Really, they don't. And if the kids don't like it – that's just tough. There *are* children who go to bed hungry at night. It's not an old wives' tale. Our children will survive a disappointing shopping trip.

The bottom line is that if we really do *have* to buy something and want to do it ethically, we will need our wits about us to achieve it. First and foremost – how do we identify an ethical product? It is no use saying that you will just trust a big, international brand. You only have to look at the travails that modern-day icons like MacDonald's, Nike and Coca Cola face.

I now spend more time examining the labels on products than I do looking at the product itself. And it can be very confusing! For instance, maybe I'm the only person who didn't understand the Mobius loop, the arrows going in a circle that you find on a lot of products. It doesn't mean that the package is 'recycled', just that it is 'recyclable'. Only if there is a percentage mentioned in the loop does it denote that a percentage of the package is made from recycled material.

And don't get me started on what recycled means! I have also discovered the huge difference between post-consumer recycled material and pre-consumer recycled material. The latter can mean as little as sweeping the floor of the pulp factory and reusing ('recycling') those woodchips which would otherwise be wasted. But the tree from which the woodchips came could have been an old growth piece of nature at its awe-inspiring best. So much for 'recycled'!

The labelling situation is improving. For food products, various organic and Fairtrade labels are widespread and credible. There is a more general European eco-label already – with stringent guidelines and enforcement.

There are also specific labels on everything from energy efficiency to forest sustainability. And we've all seen dolphin-friendly canned tuna labels. The website developed as a companion to this Guide, www. nobelmums.com, identifies many of the labels you can presently look for, dealing with the various ethical and environmental aspects of a product.

As it stands, if we stick to buying stuff that we know for a fact to be ethical, more often than not we will be walking out of shops empty-handed. Not the worst thing in the world.

It is also worth mentioning that it is mass manufacturing

that is the key environmental problem. If you are purchasing a piece of original art, the fact that it is not painted on recycled paper is not a big deal. Likewise, this Guide is *not* a call to boycott 'Made in China' goods. The burgeoning Chinese economy is lifting millions of people in China out of poverty. Our ethical product selection is a tactic to make sure that manufacturers understand that we want sustainable products. Many ethical manufacturers do source products in China – they just ensure compliance with environmental standards. We want them all to do that.

Scaling Up

The next question is "scaleability".

We know what we want to achieve – to buy less and to buy ethically (from an environmental and human rights point of view). How to go about it in a way that entices others to come along for the ride?

Barter or Borrow

We all like new stuff. It's fun. It distracts us from the fact that our way of life is unsustainable. A good way of getting the hit without generating any new factories is to exchange stuff. One possibility is to pass on toys. Every month, select five toys and meet a group of women, each with five toys. Put them in a heap and pick five that you know your kids will like. Good toys will circulate forever. As for the bad toys, at least no one in the group will need to make the same dodgy purchase.

Alternatively, open a toy library. For a small sum, families could come in and rent a toy for a month. This is definitely scaleable. Apparently, it is being done in quite a few countries already.

And what about all the grown up toys? There are so many things we each have one set of where the entire neighbourhood probably only needs a couple – do we each need a ladder, toolkit, garden mower etc.? My husband tries to move house every time enough light bulbs have popped to plunge the family into the darkness – but you should see our toolbox!

Lobbying

We can lobby manufacturers, importers, shops and governments to impose stringent and monitored labelling. And we can make sure our point is echoed by our wallets.

Accurate and comprehensive labelling, with all the audit and enforcement requirements this entails, may seem like Soviet-style bureaucracy. I wish I could think of a better way. In fact, maybe you can and that is what your Nobel will be for. In the meantime, I think we have to assume that products are unsustainable and exploitative unless there is a guarantee to the contrary. If that were not the case, we mothers would not be in a constant panic about the future of our children on an ailing planet. If, as individuals and groups of like-minded mothers, we absolutely do not buy anything without proper environmental accreditation – two things will happen. Products will be labelled to our satisfaction and manufacturing processes will improve dramatically.

A Small Business

Finally, if it is difficult to get your hands on Fairtrade, organic or otherwise ethically-labelled products – start a small business. The Internet is a viable shop front. Because of the mummy network, you should be able to publicise the selection of products that you have imported. Start on a small scale – even just buying in advance what you and your family and immediate friends need. There is no way you can sensibly import an entire range of ethical products – pick something you feel strongly about: Fairtrade, wooden toys or biodegradable nappies. By definition, what you are providing will be quality products. Your market will grow. Next thing you know, large corporations will be trying to buy you out! That's what happened with The Body Shop after all.

I can't promise that these small ethical business ventures will turn into international icons. But you would have fulfilled a growing need, made a bit of money and most importantly, signaled to big manufacturers and suppliers that there is a market for ethical goods in your neck of the woods.

Have a Eureka Moment

The other possibility is to invent something. It was a concerned mother who invented the first biodegradable nappy. If you see a need that is being filled by something environmentally unfriendly – and for which there is currently no replacement product, feel free to invent it. As mums at home, we are in a very good position to spot these gaps in the domestic consumer market after all.

As for the Nobel Prize? If you fill a need for ethical goods in your region, develop a new model to promote ethical consumerism, invent the next ethical 'mousetrap' or create the next Amazon for ethical goods, I think you have a very good chance indeed of winning that Nobel Prize someday!

"I know they are all environmentalists. I heard a lot of my speeches recycled."

(Jesse Jackson)

Chapter 7 – Spoilt for Choice – Recycling

Have you ever thought about where the rubbish goes? Imagine the fridge you threw out last week, the computer you upgraded, the toys you cleared out of the attic and binned and the takeaway you ordered last night with its ubiquitous plastic, throwaway packaging. Don't forget the disposable nappies. Now dig a large hole in the garden and put all the rubbish in it. If any of it had been bio-degradable, you would now have a very nice compost heap with which to fertilise the plants.

Unfortunately, everything you chucked out this week (except the leftover lasagna) will be with you in the garden till hell freezes over. (With recent climate anomalies that time might not be as far away as we think.) Some of it, like the batteries, might also be leaking dangerous chemicals. You might soon have a dead zone in the garden and will need to tell the children to play somewhere else.

Real life is not that different. When that fancy truck (we have a red one) comes along and collects the rubbish – all it does is take it to a hole in the ground somewhere. These are known as landfills. It sounds so innocuous, as if we were just replacing some earth with some other harmless stuff. Far from it – we are filling up every crevice of our planet with plastic crap. It is easy to avoid thinking about it once the garbage truck has been and gone – but what we are doing is no different from burying the stuff in the garden. Only we are burying it in all of our gardens.

What we can do as Individuals
Repair

Even before we recycle, there is a lot we can do to increase the lifespan of our possessions. First and foremost, we need to prolong the life of our gadgets. The problem is that replacements are so inexpensive.

My kettle was looking rather nasty, so I chucked it out and bought another. It was so cheap (about US$10). It was just not worth trying to get rid of the sediment that had built up. Or so it seemed at the time. Now I hate myself and have visions of it sitting pretty on top of a landfill somewhere waiting to take its revenge on my children. And that kettle will certainly be around long after my carbon form has turned into fertiliser.

The reason the replacement kettle was so cheap is that the cost to the environment of the revengeful original kettle, not to mention the harmful process of making me a new kettle, have not been factored into the price. It seems certain that we are not going to save the whales, our children or the planet unless people like me stop chucking out our old kettles.

Re-use

While out buying the kettle, I found myself picking up a set of spice jars. I have a weakness for rows and rows of pretty spice jars. From the moment I got home, I kept falling over small glass bottles I could have used instead. If one walks around the house with a creative and beady eye, there is so much to re-use: plastic bottles as bath toys; shoeboxes as alternate Ikea storage containers. You can even give it a fancy Ikea-style pseudo-Scandinavian name if you like – Bokst?

Recycle

This can mean a step before sorting our rubbish into different bags for the garbage collectors. You can recycle your possessions amongst your friends, have garage sales of white goods or send toys to children's charities. Basically, we need to try and get the maximum usage out of every single thing we own. The energy to produce that item has already been used. It is too late to change that. But if we prolong its life, we prevent replacements being made and bought as well as postpone the moment when it ends up in a landfill.

The final piece of the jigsaw is to recycle diligently. This means doing the sorting and binning wherever you live to make sure that the rubbish is processed and re-used.

It is important to prolong the life of an item, even where you would otherwise recycle it, because the recycling process itself involves significant energy use. The plastic bottles have to be collected, sorted, boiled or flattened or whatever they do and the recycled material must be sold to manufacturers who then refashion it into something else. Recycling is still much better than generating *new* products and packaging from raw materials. No trees are cut down. And the sum of plastic rubbish floating around remains the same. But it is important to remember that there *are* still environmental costs associated with the recycling process.

As individuals, we need to look for recycled products (remember the Mobius loop), recyclable products, use the products for as long as humanly possible in the capacity they were designed for as well as any new use we can come up with, repair it when it goes bust, flog it off to the neighbours or give it away to charity and finally – when all other options are exhausted – recycle the damn thing. With luck we will buy it back in some other form a few months hence and never be the wiser.

We can also try and buy *biodegradable* products. Biodegradable means that whatever it is you just bought won't be around till the end of time – unlike a plastic supermarket bag.

Actually, it is a bit more complicated than that. For biodegradable products to be genuinely sustainable they need to biodegrade into naturally occurring substances, without producing toxic byproducts, and this process must happen in a relatively short, 'natural' time frame. Two factors can make inherent biodegradability inherently meaningless. First, that we chuck out so much stuff that the micro-organisms that break down the product go on strike. Second, we chuck our biodegradable stuff into a landfill that does not have the bacterial activity that breaks the stuff down. Biodegradable is still better than non-biodegradable. But we still need to be buying less and making sure we dispose of it properly.

If you are not sure that recycling and biodegradibility are important, let me put it this way. The first plastic substance was invented in 1907 by Leo Hendrik Baekeland. Since that time, *every* single plastic thing we have used and thrown out is still with us somewhere – in the landfills, waterways, oceans and forests – except for that which we expressly, consciously recycled. One hundred years of plastic rubbish. It almost doesn't bear thinking about. But we have to think about it for the sake of our children.

Scaling Up

As a mother, it seems to me that the best bet is to encourage other individuals to recycle and to encourage manufacturers to use recycled products. We could do the former through cooperative structures such as a monthly garage sale where everyone brings used goods for sale or a collection point for old clothes and toys to be transported to a charity.

We could lobby for change by starting a letter campaign (on email or recycled paper) demanding that service providers such as high street banks convert paper use to recycled paper or face a boycott – especially if they are the sort that send you glossy flyers in the mail every day. We could certainly write in to the hundreds of monthly consumer magazines and ask for assurances that their paper is from sustainable forests or recycled. If they are not or refuse to tell you, boycott the magazine and make sure they know why. Lobbying for greater use of recycled products can certainly include the packaging. Biodegradable plastic bags are now available – we should lobby for supermarkets to change to those (some already have and should be rewarded with our business). If the cost is higher, we should be willing to pay a few cents extra to avoid the mountains of plastic bags clogging drains, lining streets and choking turtles and dolphins at sea.

We could identify household products that use recycled packaging or are otherwise "green" and start spreading the information to friends and mothers' groups. The next step would be to encourage supermarkets to clearly mark these products or *shelve them separately* so that the business of shopping for sustainable products is easier.

It is very important that you publicise your successes in getting manufacturers and suppliers to switch to green products as it might promote good behaviour on the part of others.

Whether your recycling strategies lead to a Nobel Prize will depend on your having encouraged recycling, promoted the use of recycled products and initiated consumer action groups. In other words, saved the planet from turning into one large garbage dump.

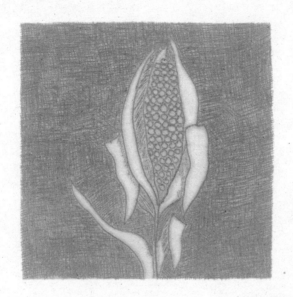

"There are people in the world so hungry, that God cannot appear to them except in the form of bread."
(Mahatma Gandhi)

Chapter 8 – Spoilt for Choice - Third World Poverty

Many of us watched Live 8.

In fact, some mothers of young children probably watched Live Aid twenty years ago in those heady, university 'change the world' days. I don't know about the rest of you but I was struck by how much more awful I felt, in a personal sense, second time around. During Live Aid, I felt empowered, individual, powerful and responsible. We were young and the sort of people we admired, anti-authority music people, were showing us that it was possible to harness the dormant sympathies of millions to feed the hungry, save lives, rescue a continent, change the world!

Twenty years later, I cried during the breaks – you know the bits where they showed us the dead and the dying and clicked their fingers – like flicking a switch and turning off the light inside another child. That was the key, I think. Having children and seeing children die.

This time around, I didn't bond with anyone. I gave away some of my husband's money. I did not think we were going to change the world, just save a few lives when the cameras were rolling. After that, it would be back to the same thing over and over again. Other people's children dying while I had a latte at Starbucks and complained about the traffic.

What a world we live in that we can buy so much, have so much and give so much to our own while others are dying. Actually dying. Not just getting by with less but dying of malnutrition and preventable diseases. The dichotomy in the reality we face, compared to the 30,000 children who die every day in the developing world, should require at the very least that we go through the looking glass to find this alternative reality. Better to go through the looking glass than look at ourselves in it.

Having had this mini-rant about our culpability, I am not sure we are really that mean or selfish or callous. Our own mental health requires that we are not constantly thinking about other people's suffering. Especially when there does not seem to be anything we can do. I am sure a lot of you donate money to charities – whether in response to specific events like the Asian tsunami or Kashmir earthquake or a general contribution to Oxfam or UNICEF. But these efforts do have that awful 'drop in the ocean' feeling at the best of times. I don't doubt we would all do more if we could find a meaningful way to do it – a mother's empathy would require nothing less.

The reason we do so little and spend the rest of the time ignoring the problem is that the roots and reasons for intense poverty are complex. Rooted in history, inflamed by the present, cross-generational, inter-cultural, multi-layered, multi-sourced – you need an MBA just to come up with enough words to describe the situation, let alone address any of the symptoms or consequences of all these ailments.

The good news is that clever, well-meaning people are making a huge effort right now to tackle global poverty. For instance, the Make Poverty History campaign has actually brought together all the disparate threads into an organised, actionable agenda. But it needs people like us to be the foot soldiers.

Basically, a number of strands need to be present before Third World poverty can be successfully challenged or alleviated:

- debt relief
- trade justice
- AIDS relief
- more aid

So what can we do? First of all, never doubt we have the power to change things. Mothers are a wonderful demographic. We cross economic, cultural and racial boundaries. One size does not fit all. As if that was not enough, we are the single global voting group that is not obsessed with the present because our primary concern is the future of our children. And finally, we have an empathy for the suffering of others – we actually care. The Americans (even George W.) understand what a powerful group mothers are or could be. That is why they are constantly obsessed with mothers as an electoral group and try to make their message as appealing as possible to 'soccer moms' or 'security moms' or whatever. Soon, I hope we will all be 'save the world moms' and politicians will have to tailor their message accordingly.

Debt relief

There are certainly steps that us stay-at-home mums can take that might make a difference. We can wear the white "Make Poverty History" wristband and lobby politicians (with letters you can find on my website, www. nobelmums.com, or links from there) to try and get the point across that we are not so selfish that we need our nation's coffers filled with the blood money of the Third World. If we can persuade our elected representatives that our vote depends on their timely action (even if you have to threaten to vote for the Monster Raving Loony Party next time out), I am sure they will be more committed to global poverty reduction.

For those who would make the point that the Third World debt money *was* borrowed, do bear in mind the principal was paid back long ago and that the interest rates are crippling. Also, the money was often lent to unaccountable governments when propping up dictators was a fashionable and 'legitimate' Cold War tactic. The dictators themselves were usually the products of brutal independence struggles against colonisation.

Trade justice

Our political systems are historically skewed in favour of the few. Rural communities from France to Japan wield far greater clout than city folk. This is because original electoral boundaries were drawn to give regions and not just individuals a say in policy-making (and urban migration has meant that relatively small communities have a disproportionate representation in parliament and government.) This is not necessarily a bad thing in itself. A strong argument can be made that countries need geographic as well as individual representation.

Sadly, this power is being used to maintain a system of farm subsidies that are destroying livelihoods in the Third World. Farmers and politicians claim that subsidies are necessary to preserve a 'way of life'. Yes, it would be nice to preserve the rolling fields of rural France and I am sure that smart farmers and their governments will find a way. But *a life* has to be more important than a 'way of life' and in this case the 'way of life' is being preserved at the expense of millions of lives and livelihoods.

Our governments appear to believe that global trade should require that Third World countries remove all barriers to entry (this is called the 'free market') while we refuse to dismantle subsidies to first world farmers. And generally speaking, these first world farmers are not brave 'sons of the soil' maintaining traditional values in a traditional society. Instead, they are large corporations that hire illegal, exploited labour to pick their crops while they perch smugly on their mountains of subsidised sugar.

What can stay-at-home mums do? We could certainly choose *not to buy* goods that are the products of First World subsidies. This is easier said than done because standard labelling only covers the country of manufacture – not the source of the underlying materials. But if we keep avoiding "subsidised" goods and also maximise the symbolic value of a boycott of particular brands – we will eventually achieve some justice for the small producers from Third World countries.

The alternative is to buy products we *know* are ethical – which might be easier than avoiding subsidised agricultural products. So for instance, if we buy cotton t-shirts from Burkina Faso and Fairtrade sugar, we know that we have refused to buy products whose competitiveness has been 'enhanced' by the economic might of the United States or the European Union.

It comes down to making an ethical choice when spending our money on food and clothes. All of us stay-at-home mums, with control over the household budget, are in a great position to make literally planet-changing purchasing decisions.

Some major brands have cottoned on (if you will forgive a pun in the midst of such a serious subject!). For instance, Marks & Spencer's are shifting to using Fairtrade cotton for various lines of their cotton apparel. We will never know whether the adoption of overtly ethical policies by mainstream brands is a matter of genuine ethics or timely marketing. I don't think it matters that much as long as the policy is not quietly dropped once the cameras have moved on. As long as the facts on the ground indicate that Third World farmers are getting the deal they deserve, providers of ethical products should be encouraged with our dollars. It's in our own interests anyway. After all, what do you think is being used to subsidise those First World farmers? It's *our* tax dollars.

And after so much of our money has been spent propping up the agricultural industries in Western countries – which in a fairer world might have made all the difference to that Burkina Faso cotton farmer and others like him – 30,000 children died today in the developing world.

Our ethical purchasing habits, harnessing the spending power of mothers everywhere, should ideally be combined with lobbying. This will speed up the process of dismantling subsidies. Otherwise, instead of recognising the error of their ways, politicians and big business will lobby harder for market access to poor countries – to dump subsidised goods there as we are not buying them anymore!

If women's groups, however small, start sending letters to their elected representatives, high street shops, magazines and newspapers (examples that you can download are on my website) demanding that we remove subsidies for our products and remove barriers to the import of Third World agricultural produce – we will collectively create a sense of momentum and might just prod our politicians to stop 'failing to find agreement' at the latest round of world trade talks.

It is, after all, almost unbelievable that the Doha round of world trade talks – which were particularly intended to address Third World poverty by reducing subsidies to European and American farmers – has not been able to reach agreement since 2001. Is it really that difficult to prevent 20% of children in sub-Saharan Africa dying before they reach the age of *five*? And if a child is dying of a preventable disease or malnutrition before he or she is five – those five 'precious' years were not pleasant.

AIDS relief

AIDS relief is harder but imperative. Many poor countries are losing their workforce to the ravages of this disease. Millions of orphans are being abandoned to rudimentary care, many of whom are HIV positive. The reality is that hardly anybody in the First World dies of AIDS anymore. Medication can prolong life and postpone the onset of full-blown symptoms indefinitely. But these drugs are patented and well beyond the reach of most Third World sufferers.

It is difficult to know what mothers are in a position to do in this context. For a start, we could lobby for aid to make these drugs more affordable. Emergency patent suspension laws and compulsory licensing of generic drugs are also possibilities. So is a little bit of generosity on the part of the pharmaceutical companies.

We could also lobby against the tying of monetary aid to notions of abstinence. It is quite possible that Laura Bush just says 'no' (I mean, who wouldn't in her place?) but I suspect it is harder for the teenage bride of the village headman to do the same.

I shall certainly preach abstinence to my children but I would not be happy with a situation where one accident, moment of weakness or stupidity would likely lead to a death sentence.

Aside from lobbying, the other possibility is trying to help the children – the AIDS orphans directly. Perhaps a community of mothers could adopt an orphanage and provide the funds to meet the needs of these children so they have some chance of a future despite a blighted past and present? Or a micro-lending scheme could be started or supported? Muhammad Yunus, 2006 Nobel Peace Prize winner, has really shown us the way with the success of the Grameen Bank in Bangladesh. Perhaps stay-at-home mums with medical or pharmaceutical backgrounds might be in a position to come up with some practical steps to help AIDS sufferers in the Third World? Channels to do some of these things already exist and are listed on www.nobelmums.com.

It is not fair that certain places are selected to have their lives improved – it is too much like playing God. But the idea would be to, as usual, find a mechanism of improvement that works and replicate it. I doubt that the recipients of much needed support whether in the form of trade justice, AIDS relief or more aid would quibble.

More aid

In the good old days, the money governments handed over as 'aid' was usually a chunk of cash given to a friendly dictator as part of Cold War efforts to maintain influence. Ostensibly for various projects, and they tended to be big infrastructure developments, the money was quickly siphoned off to Swiss bank accounts without much inquiry on the part of 'donors'. After all, it kept the dictator on side even if his citizens were still dying of hunger.

Even now, government spending on aid in many countries is tied to politics. The US gives the largest chunk of its foreign aid to Israel. They really need a lot of money – otherwise how to free up the cash to buy the weaponry to flatten small neighbouring countries? The other big recipients of US aid are Egypt – an arrangement dating back from the Camp David accord in 1978, and Iraq, for obvious reasons.

Fortunately, the international aid organisations like UNICEF and Oxfam are relatively efficient and accountable. Other charitable ventures like the Gates Foundation are becoming very creative in their aid delivery mechanisms. The good news is that this means that as long as you pick your recipient institution with some care – the money you give will be well spent.

The next question is how much ought we to give? As much as we can afford, of course. From my own experience I know that, tsunami appeals aside, it is difficult to commit to regular contributions – who knows when one might need the money? We really must try and keep in mind that, whatever we might need that money for, it is unlikely to be to prevent our children from dying before they're five. And as 1.3 billion people live on less that US$1.00 a day and 3 billion (half the population of the planet) live on less than US$2.00 a day, you will not have to give up that much to make an impact.

My suggestion is that we hand over 0.7% of our household pre-tax income to an international poverty relief fund. Consider it an addition to your tax bill and make arrangements to have it deducted every month from your bank account. Why that figure? Because that is the minimum, 0.7% of national income, our governments *first* agreed to deliver in aid in 1970. In 2005, total aid from the 22 richest countries to the world's developing countries was just US$106 billion – a shortfall of US$119 billion dollars from the 0.7% promise. On average, the world's richest countries provided just 0.33% of their

GNP in official development assistance. The United States provided just 0.22%. Perhaps we can shame our leaders into keeping their promises if we show them the right example.

We mothers spend so much time nagging our kids to share their toys, be unselfish with their siblings and to be gentle with small children. I believe that we owe it to our children to set the right example by caring about other people's children too.

There are many committed people tackling issues of poverty in developing countries. The size of the task means that every single one of us can make a contribution. And if we manage to engage ordinary people (i.e. our fellow mothers), in relevant projects whether it is to 'adopt' an AIDS orphanage, lobby for debt relief or trade justice or just commit to the 0.7% *minimum* donation – we might just make a difference – and win that Nobel Peace Prize too.

"I think—tide turning—see, as I remember—I was raised in the desert, but tides kind of—it's easy to see a tide turn—did I say those words?"

(George W. Bush)

Chapter 9 – Spoilt for Choice – War of the Worlds

It would be great if this Guide did not need to address the traditional route to the Nobel Peace Prize – dispute resolution. It would be very satisfying if the issues we had to address were limited to those where a stay-at-home mum has a special empathy or a special skill.

Indeed, I do not intend to address specific conflicts. My aim has been to make this Guide applicable to stay-at-home mums wherever they happen to be. The common thread is our common experience, not our common location.

As such, the simmering war in Sri Lanka, the breakdown of order in East Timor, the madness of Mugabe or the genocide in Sudan are not offered up individually as possible matters for mothers. This does not mean we should ignore them. But these conflicts have geographical constraints. In the circumstances, as individuals, our best hope is to convince our governments to take concerted action – ranging from sanctions to humanitarian intervention. In a different era, I would have been keen on 'regime change' in Sudan or Zimbabwe but the Iraq war has demonstrated the folly of cowboy coalitions. The United Nations must develop a framework for effective intervention in extreme situations. But the cowboys have a veto so this is not going to happen anytime soon.

There is, however, one 'war' that has touched all our lives, the ubiquitous 'war on terror'. A Guide for stay-at-home mums on how to win a Nobel Peace Prize and safeguard our children has to address such a major threat to our welfare.

The War on Terror

As a non-Moslem who grew up in a Moslem country, I feel well-placed to address the 'war on terror'. First and foremost, there isn't a 'war on terror' except in the minds of those of our leaders who like to dress up in camouflage and play at being soldiers.

Boys playing with guns will not be a sight to surprise most mothers. My own two year old can make shooting noises while pointing pens at people – and he is not allowed to watch violent television and has never had a toy gun (hence the pen). So I have no idea where he gets this intemperate streak. By comparison to my older daughter, the young fellow is much more likely to lose his temper, act violent, settle arguments by violence, try and intimidate other little boys (or be intimidated by them). He is testosterone fuelled. And in case this sounds like he should be in therapy – in his favour he will occasionally listen to reason, adores books and is gorgeously spontaneous and affectionate most of the time. And he loves animals.

Eventually, by sending him to his room regularly and talking him down as often as I can – I hope that my son will make me proud as a valuable member of society. I don't know that I will succeed, but I do know that I have to try. Like all mothers, I know that violence is not a viable method of dispute resolution. One of the underlying reasons for this, in addition to the hippy stuff, is a fear that our sons will eventually encounter a bigger, beefier young man and come off the worse from such an encounter.

Unfortunately, George W. and his brave gang of duck shooters think that there is no bigger bully in the playground (and that there will never be one) and this is the root of their aggressive posturing. If you don't think the chickens are coming home to roost, there is no incentive to be moderate in your behaviour or attitudes. You still don't have a war on terror – but what you will almost certainly have at the end of it is a violent clash of peoples and cultures.

I was pregnant with my first child when I switched on the television and saw the planes hitting the Twin Towers. I remember clearly the horror of those moments. I was terrified at the thought of bringing a child into a world where such cruelty was possible.

But at the end of the day, Osama bin Laden is no different from the Unabomber or Timothy McVeigh or any other murderer. The difference is largely one of scale. But instead of pursuing Osama bin Laden as a criminal, the Bush administration decided that they would rather play soldiers than cops and so they turned his pursuit into a war.

And by assuming/pretending/believing that all the different conflicts, so long as they tangentially involve Moslems, whether from Iraq to Afghanistan or from Lebanon to Syria, are based on the same problem – 'Islamic fascism', 'fundamentalist Islam' or whatever the label of convenience is at any given moment (all are apparently determined to set up an Islamic Caliphate from Spain to Indonesia), the Bush administration is on the verge of *creating* that which it is purporting to defeat. George W.'s straw man is now a Frankenstein's monster.

All the Moslems I know were shocked and sympathetic when the Twin Towers were destroyed. But by tarring every Moslem with the same brush as the hijackers, by invading some Moslem countries (Afganistan, Iraq), by threatening others (Iran, Syria), by killing Moslems and facilitating their killing by others (Iraq, Afghanistan, Gaza, West Bank, Lebanon) including thousands of women and children, by propping up Moslem dictatorships (Saudi Arabia, Pakistan), by incarcerating Moslems without trial (Guantanamo), by torturing some on TV (Abu Ghraib), and no doubt hundreds in secret and secreting others to repressive regimes to be tortured, many in the Moslem world are now convinced that there *is* a war on. Not a war on terror but a war on Islam or Moslems.

And they are fighting back. And the only way they see to make their attackers feel their pain is to attack civilian populations (as it is by and large Moslem civilians who are bearing the brunt of the war on terror and George W. does not get out much anyway).

And we need only be unlucky, as others have been before us, and we will be caught in the crossfire.

What we can do as Individuals

Mothers are very good at dispute resolution. We are in a constant state of peacemaking: between our children, between our children and their friends, between the kids and the neighbours, between our husbands and our mothers. And we are naturally good adjudicators as well, always seeking the 'fair' solution and not trying to maximise the spoils of victory for any one party. We are honest brokers with a real instinct for compromise. But we also have the strength, when occasion demands, to cut the Gordian knot. For instance, when the issues have become so entangled and lost in time that only a firm, even-handed 'no fault' approach can achieve peace.

Despite these strengths, we mothers are unlikely to be summoned anytime soon to replace one of those grey men in grey suits, the 'special envoys' to whatever happens to be the crisis of the moment. So what can we do?

Our best bet, to keep our children from being caught up in an episode of random violence spawned by a comic book foreign policy (the 'war on terror' against the 'axis of evil'), is to use our collective influence. We need to tilt the debate by sheer weight of numbers.

We could for instance:

- march at every peace demo we can find;
- vote (US/UK/Australia) to get rid of those who started this; and
- reach out to Moslems, especially our fellow mothers.

Outreach is critical. We cannot lock ourselves away and pray that we and our children never catch *that* plane. We must try and interact with Moslems, to demonstrate that we are people, not ciphers. Or worse, foot soldiers in this conflict foisted upon us.

All my life, I have had Moslem friends, neighbours and even mentors. The fact that they were Moslem was a non-issue. They were just people we knew, visited, played with as children. The sound of the dawn prayers on loudspeakers from the neighbourhood mosque was actually rather beautiful.

Now Moslems all over the world watch their fellow Moslems die, they believe killed for no other reason than their faith. Their anger and fear is mounting. I am hoping, perhaps naively, that a memory of a non-Moslem friend – a brief flashback of common humanity – will turn them back from doing something desperate.

As things come to a point where the world is dangerous for *all of us all of the time* and not just some of us some of the time, the political will to resolve some of the long standing issues might soon exist.

I cannot believe that the Palestinian question, the root of a lot of the distrust and suspicion in the Moslem world, will not be resolved. The 'just' solution is fairly clear after all (don't politicians watch *The West Wing*?); two states, pre-1967 borders, no refugee right of return, monetary compensation instead, East Jerusalem to the Palestinians.

All it requires is legions of mothers to lean on their governments to force the parties to accept a deal. A good start would be to deprive *both* parties simultaneously of aid, arms and holiday visas until they agree. After that, the world must pour money into the reconstruction of Palestine so that everyone is busy and happy. There will always be a few contrarians on each side who might resort to violence or at least try. But in the absence of popular support, these individuals will not amount to movements or organisations or freedom fighters or terrorists. No society is devoid of criminals and that is all any of these people would be.

In a sense, we might actually end up having to thank George W. one day. By implementing such a desperately incompetent foreign policy in pursuit of his 'war on terror', the world might actually have to *solve* some of the festering problems of the Middle East – postponement and containment no longer appear possible.

Scaling up

Well, instead of just inviting your Moslem neighbour to dinner, have a picnic for the whole street. Instead, of sending your children to play soccer at expensive training academies, send them to the nearest multiracial playground. Find funding for sports days and futsal tournaments and invite teams from different areas with a different racial and ethnic mix. Eliminate language barriers. Volunteer to be an English teacher at community centres in minority areas. Begin community anti-war initiatives. If you belong to a religious outfit, set up some sort of dialogue group. Learn Arabic.

Finally, and most importantly, even if you have never met a Moslem in your life, please don't assume that everyone with a beard or a headscarf is after you. That's like assuming that every white man with a beer gut and a tattoo is a rampaging English football fan or every black man with a gold chain is a drug pusher. Instead, let's all seek out what we have in common.

Otherwise, we will be defined by our differences and our children will reap what we sow. There is no other possible route than engagement. This is not a war that can be won by force of arms. It is no more possible than solving global warming by a 'war on weather'. Boys with toys are not going to make the world safe for our children. We mothers are going to have to step in.

Besides, if you fix some part of our broken civilisation, your Nobel is pretty much guaranteed.

"Peace is its own reward."
(Mahatma Gandhi)

Chapter 10 – Conclusion

It may seem necessary for the sake of our sanity to pretend that, if not part of the solution, at least we are not part of the problems discussed in this Guide. Unfortunately, everything we do, but especially everything we buy, does contribute – whether we are talking about global warming or global poverty. And our defensive mechanisms, shopping therapy and indulging our own children (to sublimate our guilt that we are depriving them of a future) profoundly aggravate almost every problem.

But if we deal with each issue in a small, honest way – doing the best that we can and encouraging others to do the same – we will eventually win our Nobel prizes and save the world as a byproduct. And the time spent lobbying, organising, writing, creating and researching will be both fulfilling and keep us out of the shops – impulse buying will be a thing of the past. Our purchases will be well researched in advance, probably over the Internet. We might even be able to get the stuff delivered and never have to subject ourselves to shiny shop windows again – not until the revolution is complete and shops stock only charming, environmentally-friendly, well-labelled ethical goods that would be a joy to purchase!

Nor am I suggesting that we will all be hermits – stuck in our homes, desperately trying not to make an unethical purchase. My hope is that many mothers will operate community-based projects from tree planting to carbon competitions, toy libraries to trade justice campaigns. Instead of that pseudo-community experience that is shopping, where we go to places where other people go and hope that participating in checkout queues makes us human, our time will be spent with like-minded people working towards similar objectives.

And you will be pleased to know – assuming that we are all doing everything possible to address the major issues confronting our generation – the work/life balance thing will iron itself out.

If we take the steps set out in this Guide, our daughters will never have to determine that their careers need to take second place to child-raising (or vice versa). And our sons will be able to spend time with their children – and not leave it to other people's daughters to bring them up.

The mothers seeking their Nobel Peace Prizes based on the advice in this Guide will soon be running business empires selling ethical products, be running charitable organisations or lobby groups, be freelance writers for glossy magazines on ethical and environmental issues and will constantly be sought after as consultants to big businesses trying to address the new developments in the mummy market.

And we will, of course, use the power wisely to dictate very attractive terms whether as employees or the bosses of these companies – extensive maternity leave, work from home, flexi-hours, childcare facilities, medical insurance. We will give the men we employ the same terms as well. We are, after all, above petty emotions like revenge. This new universe will be a wonderful place that allows mothers to contribute to society using the full range of their talents without compromising on the welfare of their children.

Our governments will be accountable and represent and implement our views because we mothers will speak with one voice about the major issues of our time. Our newspapers and magazines will be printed on recycled or sustainable paper and help us identify projects that need our attention while abandoning the blanket coverage of celebrity nobodies – because we won't buy them otherwise. Everyday, there will be a new story to gladden the heart about poverty reduction and community relations.

Sounds like a pipedream? Don't believe that the Nobel Peace Prize might sit on your mantelpiece some day?

Honestly speaking, you may be right. But it won't matter. If we each take the individual steps set out in this Guide and scale up as best we can – we mothers will lead fulfilling lives notwithstanding those abandoned careers. Our commitment to being stay-at-home mums will not be compromised. As the kids grow older we will have viable alternatives to belatedly rejoining the workforce. We will set the best possible example of personal responsibility to our children and we will probably save the planet and its people (not to mention the polar bears). Our children will inherit the world that they deserve. We would have saved the future. I guess we can live with that even if the Nobel Peace Prize itself does not punctuate our achievements. It is not a bad result for a bunch of stay-at-home mums.

www.nobelmums.com

I have set up a website at www.nobelmums.com. The site has information on each issue addressed in this Guide including links to other useful sites, a list of valuable reading material, downloadable template letters to send to everyone from government to manufacturers and contact details.

The site also includes a list of ethical items/brands one can already purchase, sorted by category, so that we can start the complicated business of buying ethically.

Finally, there is plenty of space on the website to take part in the stay-at-home mum revolution! Do send in any ideas you have to make a difference – or even any problems you see that you would like help from other mums with – related of course to the big issues of our generation. You can also sign up to receive emails alerts – for instance if we find another widely available ethical product or someone sends in a brilliant idea that deserves the widest circulation.

I am hoping that, via the website, we will eventually create a community of mothers with lofty ideals – and the energy and enthusiasm to achieve those ideals. I do believe that no contribution is too small, no idea is too limited and no effort is wasted in this task we have set ourselves. So do sign up and let's get this planet sorted!

A Note from the Author

I am an ordinary stay-at-home mum with very little free time. I am also the last person in the world to worry about big picture issues. And I love to shop. So when I woke up one morning and realised that my happy, healthy children were facing a very bleak future, I panicked. I started to do a lot of reading on every subject from global warming to global poverty. But most of the books were really dry and detailed – written by people and for people who were already aware of the issues and needed to know the *detail* of what to do to fix them. I came away in a state of shock, overwhelmed by the scale of the problems, uncertain of my own ability to make a difference – and needing to shop to forget.

I started doing some of the things described in this book – trying to recycle, buying only if I knew the origins of a product were squeaky-clean and even started a small business selling Fairtrade-certified products. The problem was that even to describe my efforts as a drop in a steadily warming ocean would be a gross exaggeration. And anything more intensive would have started to encroach on my time with my children and affected my *primary role* as a stay-at-home mum.

The solution was obvious. The problems we face are not unique to me. My concern for my children is certainly not an individual trait. Most other mothers are just one very hot day away from panicking about climate change or just one famine-related news item away from donating the family home to charity. And so I wrote this Guide. I hope it helps.

S Mahadevan Flint

acknowledgements

This book could not have been completed without the assistance of my mother, the support of my husband and the inspiration of my children. With special thanks to Kristine Kraabel.